Wealth Health And Everything Else

Cherlene Adewunmi

© Copyright 2025 **by Cherlene Adewunmi and CAE Publications**- All rights reserved. It is illegal to reproduce, duplicate, or transmit any part of this document in either electronic means or printed format. Recording of this publication is prohibited. Scripture reference from KJV, NIV and NLT. Dictionary references from Merriam Webster Dictionary.

Introduction

This book emphasizes taking tangible steps rather than making excuses. It requires you to utilize your time as a valuable resource and to ensure your body is functioning at optimal levels, a vessel of multiplication that God has created.

Whether you are a life coach or and a business coach, this resource provides you with the insight you need to soar.

In this book, you'll find tons of exciting business ventures to explore. The goal is for you to reflect on your passions, skills, and talents, mapping out the areas where you want to invest your time and energy, the arenas you truly enjoy!

Table Of Contents

Introduction ii

Chapter : Destiny Mapping 1

Chapter 2: Prioritize Your Time 6

Chapter 3: Tithe - Offering - Budgeting 11

Chapter 4: Write Your Way to Wealth 15

Chapter 5: Life and Business Coaching Services - Products 23

The Business of God's Prophets 30

CHAPTER 1

Destiny Mapping

A Guide to Enlarge Your Territory

And Jabez called on the God of Israel, saying, "Oh that Thou wouldest bless me indeed and enlarge my borders, and that Thine hand might be with me and that Thou wouldest keep me from evil, that it may not grieve me!" And God granted him that which he requested.

1 Chronicles 4:10

Welcome to Destiny Mapping! The purpose of this exercise is to help you see your potential, discover your greater purpose, and clarify the vision you were created to live out. This exercise delves deep into your physical being, your traumas, your gifts, your talents, and your skills. When you gain clarity on your purpose, you'll be more intentional about how you live each day, whether that's in your relationships, your business, your career, or your finances and investments. You create a beautiful life when you flow from who you truly are in God.

Getting Started

Before you begin, find a quiet space where you can reflect without distractions. Grab a notebook or open a document on your computer. Take your time with each question; this is about uncovering your true self and purpose. Now, let's dive in!

Reflection Questions

Your Major Gifts:

List five of your major gifts—those things you naturally excel at. Think about what comes easily to you, what others often compliment you on, or what you truly enjoy doing. Examples might include math, communication, writing, or artistic skills.

Exciting Aspects of the Business World:

What aspects of the business world excite you and align with your strengths? Is it administrative work, leadership, business development, marketing, or something else? Write down at least five areas that spark your interest.

Traumas and Challenges:

Reflect on the traumas you have dealt with in your life. This could include experiences from childhood to the present. Acknowledging these moments can help you understand your journey better.

Greatest Experiences:

What are some of the greatest experiences you've had in life, from childhood to now? Think about the moments that made you feel alive, fulfilled, or truly happy.

Life Accomplishments:

List five things you want to accomplish in your life. These could be personal goals, professional milestones, or dreams you've held close to your heart.

Biggest Career Goals:

What are your biggest career goals? Consider where you see yourself in the next five, ten, or even twenty years. What do you want to achieve in your professional life?

Self-Confidence and Fears:

On a scale of one to ten, how confident are you in yourself? Reflect on your regrets and fears. What holds you back, and what do you wish you could change?

Take your time with these questions. The insights you uncover will be invaluable as you embark on this journey of self-discovery and purpose. It's not just about the answers you write down; it's about the journey of reflection and understanding that will guide you toward your destiny.

CHAPTER 2

Prioritize Your Time

Each day is to be structured to help you stay focused and productive while nurturing your body and spirit. Use this schedule as much as possible, and you'll start to see your dreams come fruition. Time blocking is a fantastic way to maximize your time, allowing you to gain more of it, while also helping you set a schedule that multiplies your money and resources.

This is your opportunity to enjoy the vacation lifestyle.

Daily Schedule

6:00 AM - 7:00 AM

Morning Prayer and Reflection

Start your day with a quiet time of prayer. Take some time to connect with the Holy Spirit and write down all the directives you receive. This will propel you to great heights.

Find a comfortable, quiet space where you won't be disturbed. Settle in with a notebook and pen. Close your eyes, breathe deeply, and invite the Holy Spirit to guide your thoughts. Write down any impressions, ideas, or feelings that come to you during this time.

7:00 AM – Breakfast

Fuel your body with a small light nutritious breakfast. This size of a meal will energize you for the busy day ahead.

8:00 AM - 12:00 PM

Work with Clients

Make sure to schedule your clients during the first time block of the day. Try to fit in as many clients as you can during this timeframe. Focus on really listening to them and providing effective solutions. This approach will help you maximize your productivity while ensuring your clients feel heard and valued. Take your time with each appointment, and remember that quality interactions can make a huge difference in their experience.

Prioritize your tasks for each client. Make a to-do list and start to keep yourself organized. Use a timer technique, like the Pomodoro Technique, where you work for 25 minutes and then take a 5-minute break to stay fresh and focused.

12:00 PM Lunch

Take a break to recharge. Enjoy a healthy lunch to keep your energy levels up for the afternoon.

Pick a meal that packs in a variety of nutrients. Think salads with lean protein, whole grains, and loads of veggies. Take a break from your work area while you eat to truly give your mind a rest.

1:00 PM - 3:00 PM

Work with Clients and Projects

This is a great time to wrap up client projects as well as your own. You can create your business plans, write out your budgets, update your calendar for the next 6-12 months, and get your food schedule and personal to-do list in order. This is your second dedicated block of time to focus on your needs, so make the most of it!

Keep your workspace organized and free from distractions. Remember to check in with your clients' progress and adjust your schedule when necessary.

3:00 PM - 5:00 PM

Follow-ups and Preparation

Use this time to follow up with clients and reach out to potential clients. Make phone calls, send texts, and create your social media posts. Make a list of all the follow-ups you need to do. Prioritize them based on urgency and importance. Prepare for the evening and set the plans for the next business day.

6:00 PM - Dinner and Cleanup

Wind down your day with dinner. Enjoy your meal and take some time to clean up afterward.

Choose a healthy dinner option that satisfies you. Consider including lean proteins, whole grains, and lots of colorful vegetables. Involve family members or housemates in the cleanup process to make it quicker and more enjoyable.

9:00 PM - Evening Prayer and Reflection

Before bed, worship, pray, meditate and Journal. Reflect on your day and jot down any new insights received from the Holy Spirit.

Create a calming atmosphere with soft lighting. As you pray, express gratitude for your day and listen for any final revelations to write down.

10:00 PM - 6:00 AM – Sleep

Get plenty of rest! A good night's sleep is important for your body's recalibration. Aim for at least eight hours of sleep to feel refreshed and ready for the next day.

CHAPTER 3

Tithe and Offering and Budgeting

You need to have a written budget that you stick to. If you want to be successful, you have to be accountable for the money you already have and the money that will come in. Many individuals pray for God to give them more money and time, but the truth is, they often don't use their money to benefit God, nor do they multiply their gifts, talents, and skills to earn more. Instead, they waste time and resources by not being productive.

If you dream of becoming a millionaire or billionaire, mastering these skills is paramount. To run a successful business, you need both a personal budget and a business budget. Think of your money flowing like the ocean, vast, clean, and clear, bringing luxury and refreshment to everyone around the world, providing food and abundant resources. That's the essence of paying your tithes and offerings!

Your tithe is 10% of what you make, not 10% of what you bring home. Tithing is the 10% off the top of your income that you give. You give it to the leader God has placed in your life. The Priest whom you receive spiritual guidance and growth from. You do not pay your tithe to those who are not equipping you; you only give it to the one God directs. When you do this, your income is no longer capped. To tithe means to sow up! Sow up high and operate without limits. If you don't know where to tithe, ask the Holy Spirit and the Holy Spirit will guide you. Tithe creates an outflow of abundance. **Give and it shall be given unto you, in God measure, God will cause others to give unto you.** This means your business streams will constantly increase. You will receive an increase in clients, business, abundance, and favor. Nothing is off limits because you are operating your finances from Heaven's point of view. This life is about you being a generational leader and a steward of all wealth. Money is a tool, not a god! Learn how to master money and you will be great at mastering life!

The first three line items on your budget should always be: tithe, offering, and self. Again, your tithe is 10% of your income. An offering is anything above that 10% that you want to give to God as a show of gratitude, love and appreciation.

Start by destiny mapping! Understand your gifts and talents, and focus on operating in them. When you operate in your gifts, talents and skills, God will multiply them. ***Your gifts, when used, will create opportunities for you and bring you into the presence of Kings.*** This is where you know that God trusts you. You'll be like the great ocean flowing, creating streams of life for everyone to enjoy. On the flip side, if you cling to your money and don't give God what belongs to God, you will end up stagnant and dark, like a pond where the fish can't thrive.

The second budget line item is the offering. An offering is given based solely on what God places on your heart to give, in addition to your tithe. There's often an urging in your spirit to give. No one has to tell you to do it; you just know it's something you must do.

The third line item is "self." Pay yourself 10%. This isn't the 10% you spend on getting your hair or nails done. When you see yourself as the business, yes, hair, nails, and clothing should be viewed as investments. But if you're just starting your business, work with what you currently have and use this 10% to kickstart your business and invest in the licensing, classes, and products you need.

Here's a sample budget. Use the same format, but at the top of your expenses, list line items for Tithe, Offering, and Self. Next, include your rent or mortgage, then your car payment, and then your phone. Prioritize stability at home before mobility; if you need a ride somewhere, you can always use one of the available car sharing services. Shelter over your head and security is a must. It's your throne of home where dreams become reality.

Take this time to use the budget and create your own. Once you can see your income and expenses clearly, make any necessary adjustments.

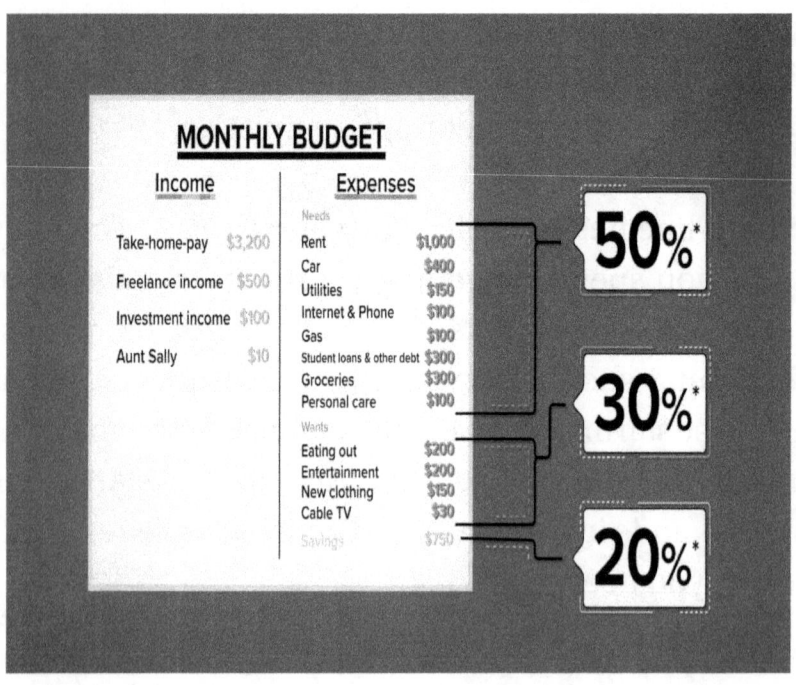

CHAPTER 4

Write Your Way to Wealth

Writing is an expansive field that encompasses a multitude of styles and formats. Whether you're an aspiring author, a seasoned professional, or just exploring writing as a hobby, it helps to understand the different forms of writing available. Make money by writing!! Here is a small list of the types of wealth streams in writing.

Life Motivations

Life motivations are often drawn from personal experiences and reflections. To write in this genre, start by identifying what drives you. Write about your passions, dreams, and the events that have shaped your life. Use anecdotes and vivid descriptions to engage your readers.

Short Stories

Short stories typically range from 1,000 to 7,500 words. To craft a compelling short story, focus on a central theme or conflict. Develop your characters quickly and build tension leading to a resolution. Remember to show, not just tell; use dialogue and action to reveal personality.

Flash Fiction

Flash fiction is a brief story, usually under 1,000 words. The challenge lies in conveying a complete narrative in a limited word count. Focus on a single moment or emotion and aim for a twist or punchline that leaves a lasting impact.

Poetry

Poetry is the art of expressing feelings and ideas through rhythm, rhyme, and imagery. To write poetry, immerse yourself in emotions or experiences and let your creativity flow. Experiment with different forms, such as sonnets or free verse, and don't shy away from using metaphor and simile.

Screenplays

Screenplays are scripts for film or television. They follow a specific format, including scene headings, dialogue, and action descriptions. To write a screenplay, focus on structure; typically, a three-act format works best. Show rather than tell through visual storytelling.

Television Scripts

Similar to screenplays, television scripts have unique formatting and pacing requirements. Write for a specific genre and consider the episode length. Character development is crucial, so create arcs that span multiple episodes.

Stage Plays

Stage plays are written for live performances. Focus on dialogue and stage directions, as the visual aspect will be conveyed through actors' interpretations. Understand the limitations of the stage and use symbolism to enhance the story.

Graphic Novels

Graphic novels combine visual art with storytelling. To create a graphic novel, collaborate with an illustrator or develop your own art. Focus on pacing and visual storytelling techniques, ensuring the images complement the narrative.

Comic Book Scripts

Comic book scripts are similar to screenplays but are formatted for panels and pages. Write concise dialogue and descriptions, and consider the pacing of the artwork. Collaborate closely with artists to ensure your vision is realized.

Non-Fiction Books

Non-fiction books explore factual topics or real-life experiences. Research extensively and organize your material into coherent chapters. Your voice should be authoritative yet engaging, guiding readers through the information.

Memoirs

Memoirs are personal accounts of significant life events. To write a memoir, choose a theme or period in your life and reflect on its impact. Use storytelling techniques to engage readers emotionally.

Self-Help Books

Self-help books offer guidance and strategies for personal improvement. Identify a specific problem and provide actionable advice. Use anecdotes and case studies to illustrate your points.

Biographies

Biographies tell the life story of an individual. Conduct thorough research and interview the subject (if possible). Organize the narrative chronologically, highlighting key events and achievements.

Travel Writing

Travel writing captures experiences in different locales. Use descriptive language to evoke the sights, sounds, and tastes of the places you visit. Include personal reflections and practical advice for readers.

Article Writing

Articles are informative pieces often found in magazines or online. Choose a topic of interest, conduct research, and structure your article with a clear introduction, body, and conclusion.

Blog Posts

Blog posts are written for online platforms and typically reflect personal opinions or experiences. Keep your tone conversational and engage readers with relevant topics. Use headings and bullet points for easy readability.

SEO Content

SEO (Search Engine Optimization) content is designed to rank high in search engine results. Research keywords related to your topic and incorporate them naturally into your writing. Focus on providing value to the reader while adhering to best practices for SEO.

Website Copy

Website copy is the text found on a site's pages. It should be clear and persuasive, guiding visitors to take action. Know your audience and highlight the benefits of your services or products.

Product Descriptions

Product descriptions provide information about items for sale. Write compelling and concise descriptions that highlight features, benefits, and unique selling points. Use persuasive language to entice potential buyers.

Social Media Content

Social media content is crafted for platforms like Facebook, Twitter, and Instagram. Keep it brief, engaging, and relevant. Use visuals and hashtags to boost visibility and interaction.

Press Releases

Press releases announce newsworthy events or updates. Keep your writing professional and succinct, following a standard format. Include a strong headline and lead paragraph to grab attention.

News Articles

News articles report current events. Focus on the "five Ws" (who, what, when, where, why) and maintain an objective tone. Use quotes and data to support your claims.

User Manuals

User manuals guide users in operating products or services. Organize content logically, using step-by-step instructions, bullet points, and visuals to enhance understanding.

CHAPTER 5

Life and Business Coaching Services and Products

Life and business coaches earn substantial income through one-on-one and group sessions, helping their clients achieve a wide range of goals.

Coaches write books, develop programs, and create curriculums that enhances the lives of their clients. They craft courses to share their insights on various subjects, including leadership, finances, business, health, wellness, family, education, stress management, and career strategies. Additionally, coaches often launch websites with exclusive content tailored to meet their clients' future needs, generating passive income. They also secure speaking engagements in both the public and private sectors. By branding themselves on social media, coaches provide valuable content to the world, establishing themselves as go-to experts in their fields.

Here are several income streams you can explore!

Personalized Budgeting Templates

Create customizable templates that clients can use to manage their finances effectively.

Debt Management Plans

Offer structured plans designed to help clients tackle and eliminate their debt.

Investment Strategy Guides

Share your expertise by crafting guides that explain various investment options and strategies.

Workshops on Financial Literacy

Host engaging workshops to help clients grasp fundamental financial concepts.

Online Courses on Retirement Planning

Develop courses that guide clients through the essentials of planning for a comfortable retirement.

One-on-One Coaching Sessions

Provide personalized coaching to assist clients in setting and achieving their financial goals.

E-books on Wealth Building

Write comprehensive e-books that cover different aspects of building wealth over time.

Financial Goal-Setting Tools

Create resources that help clients define and track their financial objectives.

Tax Planning Resources

Offer materials that guide clients through effective tax planning strategies.

Monthly Subscription Services for Ongoing Guidance

Provide a subscription model that delivers continuous support and advice to clients.

Career Coach Products

In the world of career coaching, having a strong suite of products is essential for helping clients navigate their professional journeys. Here's an overview of valuable services that can make a difference:

Resume Writing Services

Crafting a standout resume is crucial for clients looking to catch the eye of potential employers. With tailored guidance, clients can develop resumes that not only showcase their skills and experiences but also reflect their unique personalities.

Interview Preparation Sessions

The interview process can be nerve-wracking, but with mock interviews and personalized tips, clients can boost their confidence and performance. These sessions focus on honing interview skills, preparing for common questions, and developing effective communication techniques.

Career Assessment Tools

Understanding one's strengths and interests is key to finding the right career path. By utilizing specialized assessment tools, clients can gain valuable insights that help them make informed decisions about their futures.

Online Courses on Job Search Strategies

In today's competitive job market, knowing effective job search techniques is vital. Creating online courses enables clients to learn at their own pace, gaining skills that will enhance their job search efforts.

Networking Workshops

Building and leveraging a professional network is essential for career advancement. Hosting workshops can empower clients with the knowledge and strategies needed to cultivate meaningful connections in their industries.

LinkedIn Profile Optimization Services

A well-crafted LinkedIn profile can open doors to new opportunities. Assisting clients in enhancing their profiles ensures they present themselves professionally and attract the attention of recruiters and potential employers.

Personal Branding Guides

Sharing insights on personal branding helps clients develop and communicate their unique value propositions. A strong personal brand can set them apart in a crowded job market.

One-on-One Coaching Sessions

Tailored coaching sessions offer personalized guidance for clients navigating their career journeys. This individualized approach helps address specific challenges and goals, fostering growth and development.

Job Market Trend Reports

Staying informed about current job market trends is crucial for strategic career planning. Providing clients with insightful reports can help them understand industry shifts and make informed decisions about their future.

Monthly Newsletters with Career Development Tips

Sending out newsletters packed with tips and resources can support clients in their ongoing career growth. These newsletters can serve as a regular touchpoint, keeping clients engaged and motivated.

The Business of God's Prophets

The Business of God's Prophets

God is all about business. Throughout the Bible, from the Old Testament to Revelation, the focus is on God's children, making sure the land and the Earth are taken care of, while also ensuring that the inhabitants honor God with their lives and enjoy the abundance God has made available to them.

Prophets play a significant role in honoring God by managing God's business. They are business leaders for God, making sure that people receive the purity, structure, and everything else God wants to provide them as they follow the blueprints laid out by God.

As God's scribes, prophets write books, compose songs, and develop curriculums. Their main goal is honoring God. Beyond teaching, they focus on building a community of congregants whom they nurture, uplift, and equip for their spiritual journeys. They create global prophetic networks and schools.

Prophets help individuals stay connected to God. They serve as teachers, preaching, prophesying, and providing guidance to help individuals live lives that please God. To further equip individuals, prophets host workshops and seminars, and they create podcasts for their ministries.

www.ingramcontent.com/pod-product-compliance
Lightning Source LLC
LaVergne TN
LVHW051807080426
835511LV00019B/3438